# TECH TYKES
by WSU TECH

# BECKHAM
## THE BIOLOGIST

# AND THE OUTDOOR ADVENTURE

BY SHEREE UTASH, ED.D AND MANDY FOUSE

# BECKHAM
## THE BIOLOGIST

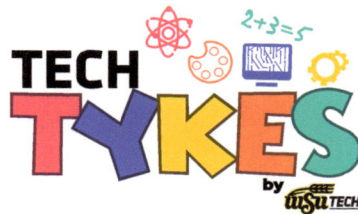

TECH TYKES
by WSU TECH

SPARKING CURIOSITY IN SCIENCE,
TECHNOLOGY, ENGINEERING,
ART, AND MATH

Illustrated by Jesús Gallardo

ISBN: 978-1-961600-08-9
Library of Congress Control Number: 2025900554

FIG FACTOR MEDIA

WSU TECH

2

To the curious minds and future innovators, this series is for you. May your imaginations soar as you explore the wonders of science, technology, engineering, art, and math (STEAM). Here's to the dreamers who believe anything is possible and the creators who will shape tomorrow's world. Keep asking questions, keep tinkering, and always stay curious. The future is in your hands! And to Grayson, Ella, Noah, Bryson, Eevy, Porter, Paisley, Emry, Beckham, and Parker—thank you for inspiring the characters that bring these stories to life.

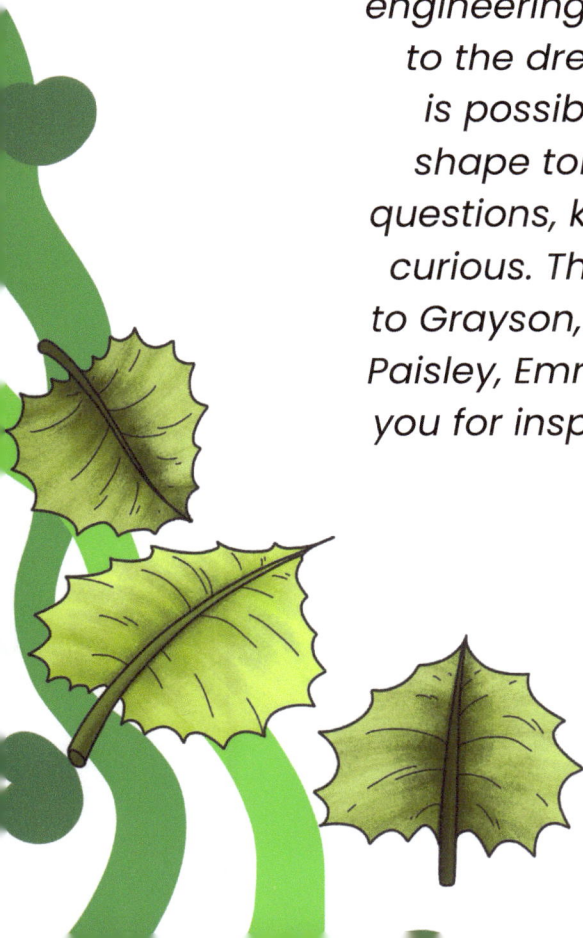

Hi, I'm Beckham. I'm nine years old. I love being outside, exploring nature, and learning about all the living things around me. I watch videos on the internet about biologists. They are people who study living things. My favorite videos are where biologists go on exciting adventures to study plants and animals. They even share tips on how kids like me can explore nature, too! I want to be just like them one day!

My little sister, Parker, loves following me on all my adventures. She may only be four and small, but she's always ready to explore with me and be helpful...well, most of the time!

I have a group of friends. We call ourselves the Tech Tykes, and we love exploring new things and going on adventures. Sometimes, even Parker joins in! We learn about all sorts of cool things, but my favorite is when we explore nature. That's the outside.

One Saturday morning, my family and I woke up super early to go on a hike. I was excited because my dad told me there was a waterfall at the end!

We packed snacks, water, towels, and my explorer kit—complete with my notebook and pencil, magnifying glass, and camera. This was my first real hike so I was nervous but I was on a mission to find and learn about as many animals and plants as possible and swim in the waterfall!

When we got to the trail (that's where you walk on a hike) I saw green trees and tall yellow grass. As we started to walk, I heard a soft croaking sound.

"Shhh! There's something here," I whispered to Parker. I carefully moved the grass and saw a bright green frog sitting on a moss-covered rock near a stream. Its skin was smooth and shiny.

"Wow, this frog is so cool!" I said, taking a picture.

"Biologists like to observe animals in their natural habitat," I told Parker. "That means we watch what they do without bothering them."

We kept walking and saw colorful flowers by the trail. The petals were bright yellow, pink, and blue. A butterfly with orange and black wings landed on one of the flowers.

"These are wildflowers," my mom said. "They provide food for bees and butterflies."

I took another picture. "Bees and butterflies help plants grow by spreading pollen," I said.

"Without them, plants couldn't make seeds."

As we hiked further, we reached a small clearing (that's an open area in the woods). There were tall trees and soft grass. My dad pointed to a deer eating leaves off a bush.

"Look at how the deer uses the plants for food," I said. "Everything in nature is connected. The plants give animals food, and the animals help spread the seeds."

**I FELT LIKE A REAL BIOLOGIST, DISCOVERING HOW EVERYTHING WORKED TOGETHER.**

As the deer walked off, I turned around and saw a new plant I had never seen. The leaves were wide and had tiny ridges. I started to draw it like I had seen other biologists do, but I couldn't get the shape right.

I felt frustrated and closed my notebook. Right then, my mom walked up.

"Even biologists don't get everything right the first time," she said. "Sometimes they use other tools to help them."

I looked at the plant again and got an idea. I put a leaf under a piece of paper and rubbed a crayon on top. When I picked up the paper, I saw a perfect leaf shape! I could even see all the little lines and edges!

"Wow, this is better than drawing!" I said. "Now I can look it up when we get home and find out what kind of plant it is."

**MY MOM SMILED AND SAID, "SEE? SOMETIMES EVEN BIOLOGISTS MUST THINK OF NEW WAYS TO STUDY NATURE."**

As we kept walking, the sound of rushing water grew louder.

"We're almost there!" my dad said with a big grin. I could feel the excitement bubbling up inside me. After climbing over some rocks and winding through the trees, we finally saw it.

There was a beautiful waterfall flowing into a clear, sparkling pool.

"Let's go swimming!" I yelled, quickly setting down my backpack.

Parker sat on a rock and pulled out a granola bar from her pocket. She unwrapped it and tossed the wrapper on the ground.

"Parker!" I said, picking up the wrapper. "You can't just throw trash on the ground."

"Why not?" Parker asked.

**"DO YOU KNOW WHAT AN ECOSYSTEM IS?" I ASKED.**

Parker shook her head.

"It's like a big puzzle," I explained. "Plants, animals, water, and even the dirt work together to keep everything healthy and growing." Biologists, especially ones who study the environment, like ecologists, work hard to understand how all the pieces of that puzzle fit together."

"But it's just a small piece of trash," Parker said.

"Trash doesn't belong in nature. It's not part of the ecosystem. Animals might eat the trash on accident and get sick, or it could block plants from getting the sunlight and water they need to grow. Ecologists study these problems and find ways to help, but the best way to protect nature is for all of us to keep it clean."

Parker's eyes got big. "So, if we don't put trash on the ground, we help the puzzle stay together?"

"Exactly!" I said.

I looked around and noticed more trash. There was a plastic bottle near a bush, a crumpled chip bag by the rocks, and even a broken sandal!

"Look at all this!" I said, pointing. "Let's be biologists and clean up the trash so the animals stay healthy and the waterfall stays beautiful."

## "OKAY!" PARKER SAID, JUMPING UP.

We used one of our empty snack bags to gather all the trash we could find. When we were done, my dad said, "Great job, you two! Now, go for a swim, and then we will take all this back to the campsite and throw it away."

Just then, I heard a splash. I turned around and saw a big bird swoop down into the water. "That's a heron!" I said, excited. "They catch fish in the water and use their long legs to walk through the marshes without sinking."

As I watched the heron fly off, I thought about how being a biologist isn't just about studying animals and plants. It's about finding ways to learn, solve problems, and understand how everything in nature is connected.

I knew that even though I was still a kid, I could make a difference, just like the biologists I watch online.

As we walked back to the campsite, we talked about how important it is to take care of the outdoors. Exploring nature is amazing, but it's even better when we protect it for all the plants, animals, and people who love it, too.

That night, around the campfire, I showed my family all the pictures I had taken and the leaf impression I had made, and Parker showed everyone the bag of trash.

**I LOOKED AT MY SISTER AND SAID, "SEE, PARKER? BEING A BIOLOGIST ISN'T JUST ABOUT LEARNING COOL STUFF. IT'S ABOUT HELPING, TOO.**

She smiled and asked. "Do you think I can be a biologist when I grow up?"

"Of course!" I said. "All you need is curiosity, patience, and a love for nature. And if we keep learning and exploring, we'll be biologists for real one day."

# ABOUT THE AUTHORS

**D**r. Sheree Utash, Ed.D., is a proud Wichitan, leader, and educator, but she's a mom, daughter, and a Gigi (grandma) first! As president of WSU Tech, she's dedicated to creating opportunities for students to achieve their dreams, but her favorite moments are spent cheering on her grandchildren and celebrating their curiosity and achievements. Sheree believes in the power of education to transform lives and communities—one learner at a time.

**M**andy Fouse is a Wichita native, communications expert, and passionate mom to two young, imaginative minds. At WSU Tech, she leads efforts to craft and share stories that inspire and connect people, showcasing the incredible work being done across the college. Mandy believes that every student and individual has a story worth telling. She works to highlight the voices of tomorrow's leaders and inspire the next generation of thinkers and doers.

*All proceeds from the Tech Tykes series will support WSU Tech's efforts to inspire and prepare the next generation of innovators, creators, and problem-solvers. Funds will be used to enhance educational opportunities, ensuring young learners have access to hands-on experiences that spark a lifelong love of science, technology, engineering, arts, and mathematics (STEAM).*

www.ingramcontent.com/pod-product-compliance
Lightning Source LLC
Chambersburg PA
CBHW041431090426
42744CB00003B/35